Contents

A **unique** collaborative project

By Juan Ignacio Vidarte, Director General of the Guggenheim Museum, Bilbao

Every project aspires to a successful maturity. After ten years in operation, there are plenty of signs to suggest that the project for the Guggenheim Bilbao has attained that desired state of consolidation. It would indeed be difficult to imagine the Biscayan capital without the Guggenheim Museum moored there on the left bank of the old thoroughfare that is the River Nervión. And yet it was only a few years ago that we were studying with a mixture of disconcertment and admiration the first models that architect Frank O. Gehry showed us of this avant-garde building that was to become the home of one of the world's most important institutions for modern and contemporary art, the prestigious Solomon R. Guggenheim Foundation.

The project to set up a new outpost of the Guggenheim Foundation in Bilbao emerged from a series of initiatives developed by the administration of the Basque province in their concern to regenerate the economic structures of the Basque Country by diversifying the activities in Bilbao beyond its traditional industrial base, and to stimulate the conversion of the Bilbao conurbation into a leading pole on the Atlantic coast. The idea that culture could be a factor for development originally met with scepticism and a degree of mistrust. But the success of the Guggenheim from its first year onward backed up this conviction. Beyond its own specific merits as a driver of creativity and consolidator of identity, culture warrants serious consideration as a strategic option in policies of economic development and urban regeneration. The history of our institution provides proof that the cultural factor was decisive in persuading businesses to set up here and as a stimulant for the growth of tourism and services and, finally, a vector to help promote the region's image abroad.

Thus the Guggenheim Museum Bilbao became a reality thanks to the exceptional collaboration between, the Basque administrations and the Solomon R. Guggenheim Foundation, based on the complementarity of their resources. The Basque administration took charge of the construction of the building and has since provided the political, cultural and financial authority to support the operation of the museum, while the Solomon R. Guggenheim Foundation has made available its collections, a number of exhibition programmes and its experience in museum organisation. This collaboration is based on a principle of mutual benefit and the need to undertake actions on an international scale.

The Guggenheim Museum Bilbao thus has the privilege, not only of being housed in an extraordinary piece of contemporary architecture, but also of having access to the essential part of the permanent collection held by the museums forming the Guggenheim network. Furthermore, the Guggenheim Bilbao benefits from the strategic alliances established by the Solomon R. Guggenheim Foundation with some of the world's most important museums, such as the Hermitage in Saint Petersburg and the Kunsthistorisches Museum in Vienna. Consequently, it is able to share resources and programmes and, above all, artworks, which help strengthen and enrich its own collections. These alliances give it a broad historical base from which to explore the foundations and key events of modern and contemporary art.

The decisive element that enabled us to carry the project through was the creation of an administrative model capable of ensuring the efficient management of resources, a quality artistic programme, visitor satisfaction and a high degree of private initiative guaranteeing a good level of self-financing. It is to this end that the Bilbao Guggenheim has initiated various programmes aimed at private and corporate members. These have brought it generous support, not only from business but also from various social organisations. Today, the Museum has more than fifteen thousand five hundred Friends and some hundred and fifty businesses and institutions make a significant contribution to financing its activities. This mixed model, which combines institutional support and private management, has proved a magnificent solution for the management of cultural organisations. ■

The Guggenheim Museum Bilbao seen from Calle
Iparraguirre, with Jeff Koons' *Puppy* sitting in front of it.

A look back
at a project

The determination and commitment of the Basque Country played a decisive role in bringing a new outpost of the Solomon R. Guggenheim Foundation to Bilbao. Here is the story of the will and the talents behind that momentous decision.

The original plans behind the creation of the Guggenheim Museum Bilbao date from the late 1980s, when the Basque authorities launched an urban regeneration programme with a view to diversifying the city's economic structure, which in those days was dominated by the legacy industries of steel and shipbuilding. This major cultural undertaking was to help inject new dynamism into the Basque Country and to help transform the Bilbao area into the hub of Spain's Atlantic regions. The outstanding element of this planned development was a museum of modern and contemporary art.

An international project

Also at the end of the 1980s, the Solomon R. Guggenheim Foundation was thinking about expanding, for its museums in New York and Venice were no longer big enough to do full justice to its collection. They first sought to create an extension in Venice, and then considered an extension in Salzburg, but negotiations failed to bear fruit. Nevertheless, these experiences had provided the Foundation with an opportunity to define what it wanted more precisely and to sketch out an international project with clearly defined museological criteria. The aim was to put its resources to work more effectively, but also to coordinate a network of institutions set up in different parts of the world. This concept stood in contrast to the traditional model of the museum, which had been increasingly challenged since the mid-twentieth century.

Carmen Giménez, who at the time was organising an exhibition of works from the Guggenheim Collection at the Museo Nacional Centro de Arte Reina Sofía in Madrid, acted as a mediator by facilitating contact between the Solomon R. Guggenheim Foundation and the directors of the Basque institutions in 1991. The directors of the American foundation were greatly interested in the proposition put to them by

Maman, a monumental sculpture by Louise Bourgeois, stands guard outside the Museum.

The footbridge over the river echoes the curves of the building.

Built on a bend in the river, the museum plays on all the site's constraints, in particular the La Salve Bridge, which Frank O. Gehry integrated into his architectural composition.

the Basque institutions. Their Spanish interlocutors were determined to create a major cultural complex, and committed to a major investment in the project. For the Solomon R. Guggenheim Foundation, setting up an important museum in Bilbao would meet the economic, political and aesthetic requirements, premised on international cultural exchange, that it had placed at the centre of its recently adopted development policy. In December of the same year, the two sides reached a preliminary agreement with a view to creating the foundation for a Guggenheim Museum in Bilbao. This body would ensure the management of the new museum as an independent institution.

An icon for our times

The Basque authorities had already chosen the site where they wanted the museum built. The architecture, it was agreed, would itself be a contemporary masterpiece, a model. The competition brought together three carefully selected architects. The winning project was the one by Frank O. Gehry. In the summer of 1993 demolition work began on the old buildings occupying the land. Soon, the first stone would be laid. The structure began to take shape in October 1994 and before the year was out the Solomon R. Guggenheim Foundation and the Basque authorities had signed the management agreement laying down the terms of their collaboration. The nature of their partnership was dictated by the complementary nature of their resources. The Basques brought to the table political and cultural authority as well as financial wherewithal, while the Guggenheim brought its expertise in museum development and the kernel of works for exhibition, taken from one of the world's finest private collections of modern and contemporary art.

Finally, on 31 December 1995, the Solomon R. Guggenheim Foundation submitted a draught of its strategic management plan for the first four years, 1997–2000, thus initiating a process of analysis and negotiation that culminated in the approval by the Executive Committee of the Guggenheim Foundation in Bilbao – set up a few months earlier – of the operating plan. This restated the initial directives establishing the functioning of the Museum. Finally, on 18 October 1997, the Guggenheim Museum Bilbao was officially inaugurated by Their Majesties King Juan Carlos and Queen Sofía of Spain.

The undeniably strong identity enjoyed by the Guggenheim Museum, Bilbao has made an important contribution to constructing and disseminating a modern, dynamic and cosmopolitan image of the Basque Country. Moreover, after ten years of activity, it occupies a leading position in the international network of Guggenheim museums. The institutions in this network share experience, resources and collections, while maintaining their complementary qualities. Bilbao has thus been able to develop its cultural heritage to an unprecedented level, while contributing to the development and artistic education of its population. The Guggenheim Museum, Bilbao has introduced the city and, by extension, the Basque Country, into the European and global art circuit, at a level of excellence and with results that it was impossible to foresee when the project began. The Museum's success has also encouraged the creation of other cultural complexes and the renovation of the existing infrastructure, so that our citizens and visitors may benefit from a rich and diverse set of cultural choices. ∎

Below: the atrium opens onto a terrace and a water garden bordering the river. In the foreground, Yves Klein's *Fire Fountain* in action.

Page right: Jim Dine, *Three Red Spanish Venuses*, 1997, polystyrene stretched over a steel framework, nylon mesh, red acrylic latex finish, three elements, each 7.62 m high.

Titanium icon

The baroque sculptural edifice dreamed up by
Frank O. Gehry for the Guggenheim Foundation in Bilbao
is a technological feat, but one that was immediately at
home in the heart of the Basque city and quickly became
its globally recognised icon.   BY JEAN-FRANÇOIS LASNIER

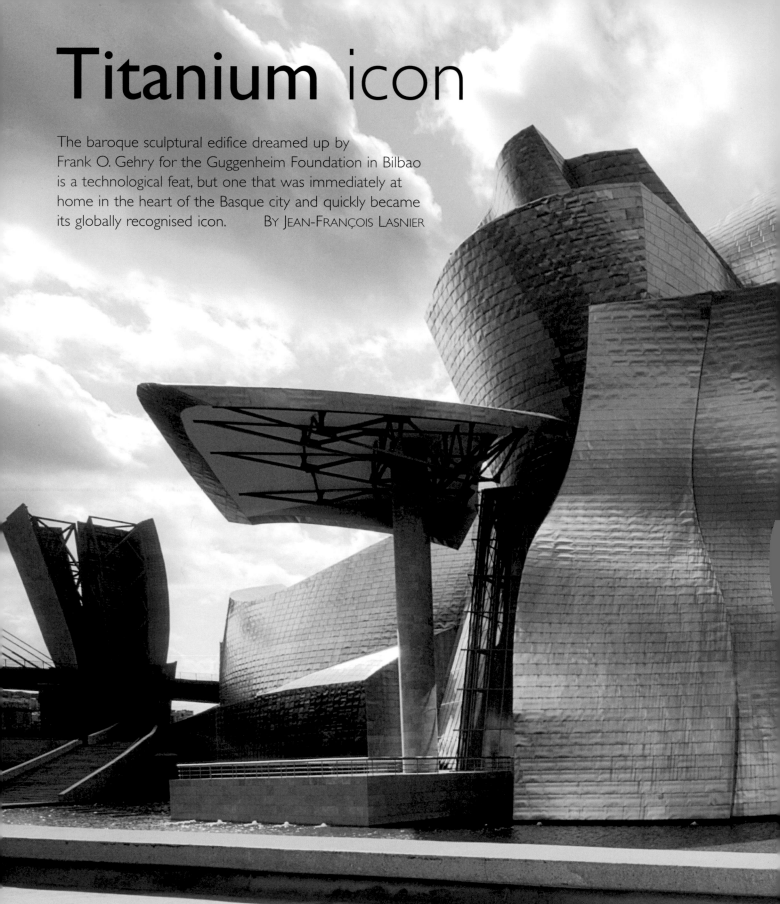

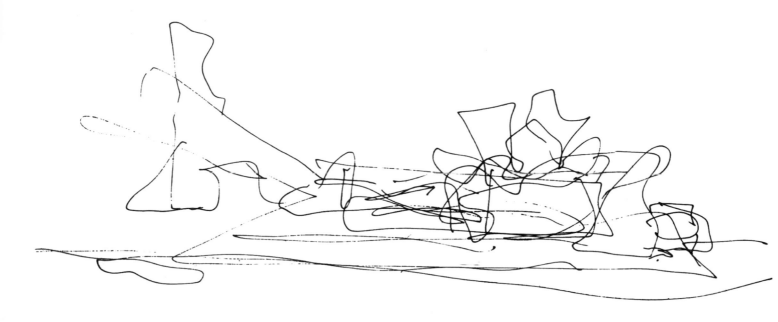

Drawing by Frank O. Gehry representing the northern
elevation of the Guggenheim Museum Bilbao, 15 July 1991,
ink on paper, 23 x 30.5 cm.

Hit hard by the deindustrialisation of the 1970s and 1980s,
Bilbao faced a stark choice: inexorable decline or radical
conversion. Economic recovery, on the back of the service
sector, would go hand in hand with an ambitious urban
regeneration programme, for the industries of yesteryear had
left behind extensive brownfield sites still encumbered by
abandoned factories and sheds. The Basque authorities had
plans to create a cultural centre in an old wine warehouse, the
Alhóndiga. Their still embryonic project now connected up
with the plans of the Solomon R. Guggenheim Foundation,
which wanted to establish a network outside the US.
However, Thomas Krens, director of the American foundation, was openly sceptical when invited to view the site.
Enter Frank O. Gehry. Sharing Krens's reservations about
the Alhóndiga, he looked instead to the old abandoned docks
on a bend in the River Nervión. Located close to the fine arts
museum, the opera and the university, here, he thought, was
a site that was just right for cultural activities.

As the location changed, so too did the project, as was clear
from the terms of the limited architectural competition that

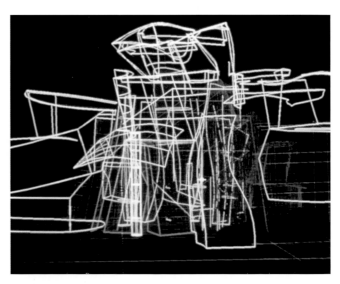

The different forms of the Museum were modelled
by Frank O. Gehry assisted by the computer CATIA,
developed by the French firm Dassault to design
fighter planes.

Frank O. Gehry constructed his simplified maquette using wooden shapes.

was now launched. In addition to Gehry, the Austrian agency Coop Himmelblau and the Japanese Arata Isozaki were also contacted. The client's goal was clear: they wanted 'a building that will be greater than the sum of its parts and will have a powerful iconic identity, so that people will want to visit it for itself while respecting the works of art exhibited there'. The implicit reference in this programme was the magical spiral of the Guggenheim Museum in New York, conceived by Frank Lloyd Wright in the 1940s and inaugurated in 1959. The other more or less acknowledged model was Sydney Opera House, the ogival shells of which had dominated the city's seafront for thirty years, making this design by the Dane Jørn Utzon the city's icon. The future museum was also part of a set of architectural commissions initiated by the local authority within the framework of a new urban policy, along with the renovation of the airport, the construction of a foot-bridge over the river by Santiago Calatrava, the conception of an underground transport system by Norman Foster and the construction of a conference centre by Federico Soriano. As it prepared for the 1992 Olympic Games, Barcelona had

undertaken an ambitious urban regeneration programme, featuring a number of prestigious architectural projects. As with the Catalans, so the feeling of Basque identity would be strengthened, not in a regionalist withdrawal, but by insisting on world-class architecture.

Drowning in the paper

The architects were given three weeks to present a project, starting on 26 June 1991. On site, Gehry made a few sketches as the basis for a simplified plan. The gestation of the Guggenheim Museum, Bilbao, which was perfectly documented, is characteristic of the architect's working process. Using a technique close to automatic writing, Gehry makes abundant drawings, or 'scribbles' as he calls them, from which the forms gradually emerge. 'I look through the paper and try to pluck out the formal idea; it's like someone drowning in the paper. That's why I don't think of what I do as designs; I can't. It's only afterwards, when I look.' Several major features of the future building took shape at this stage, from the flower-shaped glass ceiling to the long

The definitive maquette complete
with the tower, February 1994.

Gehry, architect and demiurge

In 1954 the young Owen Goldberg, born in Toronto in 1929 into a Jewish family from Poland, changed his name: from now on he would be called Frank Owen Gehry. But Gehry did not become Gehry, the architect and demiurge, until 1978. When building an extension to his home in Santa Monica, he engaged in some very novel spatial and material experiments which aroused the interest of critics. He was nearly fifty, and a new career beckoned. After years of erratic activity, commissions bloomed and project followed project: museums, apartment buildings, offices, auditoriums, etc. In 1989 he secured his reputation and won the prestigious Pritzker Prize when he built the Vitra Design Museum at Weil am Rhein. His plans for the Walt Disney Concert Hall in Los Angeles were ready in 1991, but his magnum opus would have to wait until 2003. In the meantime he built the Guggenheim Museum in Bilbao, which is in many respects similar. Gehry is now at the head of an agency of 175 men and women, but continues to play a hands-on role in every one of its projects.

A panoramic view from Mount Artxanda.

gallery inspired by the hull of a ship. In many of his projects Gehry pushes his sculptural images to such a high degree of abstraction that the only things left are values and sensations attached to figures – fluidity and continuous movement, for example, being all that he kept from the snake image. At the Walt Disney Concert Hall in Los Angeles, the plans for which he was finalising at the time, Gehry was thinking of images of sailboats. 'I was simply trying to create an impression of movement with my buildings, a kind of subtle energy. And I like to create a building that gives an impression of movement because it fits in with the wider movement of the city, and it changes. There is something transient about it.' These words neatly sum up his approach to the Bilbao Guggenheim.

The forms that arise from the 'scribbles' were transformed into simplified models: on top of the geometrical masses he added the more freely formed flower of the metal, setting up a tension between fragmented volumes, of the kind he had experimented with at the Vitra Design Museum in Weil

am Rhein and at the Frederick R. Weisman Museum in Minneapolis. For his 'petals' he unhesitatingly borrowed from another ongoing project, a skyscraper in Los Angeles. Then the tower took up position on the other side of the bridge, linked to the Museum by a long gallery.

Concrete questions

The jury met on 20 and 21 July 1991 and chose Gehry's project. They appreciated the way he used materials characteristic of the site, as well as the interaction between the spaces, the presence of big exhibition halls and the building's integration into its setting. But they also had their reservations about his design: Was a tower really necessary? What was its function? Where exactly would the entrance be? Such were the concrete questions the architect had to answer in the next phase. A feasibility study carried out in 1992 would also specify the contents of the artistic project and the construction costs. This study also defined the area – 24,000 square metres – and the ratio of gallery to service

Page left: the Guggenheim Museum Bilbao under construction.

Above: the building is clad in limestone, glass and, above all, titanium.

space, 1:2. As the remit gained in detail, so did Gehry's ideas as he moved continuously between sketches and models in order to respond to the various requirements formulated by Thomas Krens, who was his main interlocutor during the completion of the definitive project.

The process leading from drawings to models, and then to the building, came up against a major difficulty: how to transcribe the products of such a fertile imagination into reality without pushing the budget sky-high? As always in architecture, technology now came to the aid of the imagination, thanks to computer software borrowed from the aeronautical industry. 'A lot of the forms he is developing right now would not be possible without computers', stressed his colleagues Randy Jefferson and Jim Glymph. 'Bilbao is a perfect example of this. Before, these forms would have been seen as something to avoid. They were good ideas as a sketch, but they were impossible to build. Bilbao could have been designed with a pencil and a ruler, but it would have taken several decades.' All the pieces in Gehry's complex metal structure were thus calibrated on the computer programme before they were manufactured.

Another key element in the genesis of the project was the choice of materials for the facade. Gehry had originally wanted to use leaded copper, but this was ruled out because

of its toxicity. As at the Frederick R. Weisman Museum in Minneapolis, completed in 1990, tests were carried out with stainless steel, but the architect was not satisfied. He now became interested in titanium: 'This metal could be both warm and characterful', he recalls. 'Titanium is finer than steel, it is a third of a millimetre thick and has a soft texture; it doesn't rest flat and the wind makes its surface ripple. These were all qualities that we learned to put to use.'

A dialogue with the urban fabric

While the Basque authorities and the Guggenheim Foundation were discussing the functioning of the future institution, the first stone was laid in October 1993. Four years later, the space at last opened to the public. The first undeniable achievement was that the new building had succeeded in entering into a subtle dialogue with the urban fabric: the expressway, the bridge, the river, the post-industrial landscape of the old harbour, and even the views from the neighbouring streets – the whole of Bilbao seemed to have entered into its formal conception. The sensitivity to context manifest in earlier projects such as the Loyola School of Law in Los Angeles had been raised to a higher level in the Basque city. For example, the big gallery that passes under the bridge and then blossoms into a tower that seems

Above: the Museum houses nineteen
galleries over three levels, around
a vast central atrium.

Page right: view of the atrium from
the second floor of the Museum.

to have split open anchors the museum to its surroundings.
As for the titanium skin, it refers explicitly to the city's industrial past and the shimmering light on its surface mirrors the
reflections on the river.

From the outside, the Guggenheim has two faces: orthogo-
nal structures in limestone, and curved volumes clad in
titanium. The organic quality of this architecture makes it a
remote descendant of the work of Frank Lloyd Wright.
Entering the Museum, it is indeed difficult not to sense the
shadow of that tutelary genius. In response to the vertiginous
spiral of the Guggenheim in New York, Gehry created an
atrium in the manner of a sculptor as much as an architect.
Pointing one day to a photograph of Brancusi's studio standing on his desk, he said: 'He has more influence on my work
than most architects.' Glass lifts, stone stair towers, curving
walkways suspended from the ceiling – the circulation

passages are presented in a kind of dream city whose curves
and vertical élan once again bring to mind organic metaphors.
In the abundant light that streams in through the flower-
shaped overhead glass and the curtain walls, flows of vital
energy seem to rise up to the sky and carry visitors into a rich
sensorial and emotional experience. The grand gallery, which
is 130 metres long and 30 wide, where Richard Serra's monumental work *The Matter of Time* is on permanent display,
extends this perception of an expanding space-time.

Commenting on Wright's Guggenheim Museum, the
visionary architect Frederick Kiesler pronounced a judge-
ment that could equally well apply to Gehry's: 'The grandeur
of this building's conception outweighs all the erring of
modern art and gives the visitor the unforgettable feeling of
having lived, if only for a fleeting moment, in a universe
created by man.' ∎

The collection of the
Guggenheim Museum Bilbao

In addition to pieces from the international Guggenheim collection, the Bilbao Museum has its own holdings, which feature major works by some of the most important artists of the second half of the twentieth century, as well as specially made pieces and other works by contemporary Basque and Spanish artists.

BY THE CURATORS OF THE GUGGENHEIM MUSEUM BILBAO

Ever since its foundation, one of the fundamental missions of the Guggenheim Museum Bilbao has been to build up its own collection. Its goal is to bring a together an ensemble of works of the first order by internationally renowned artists from 1945 to the present. Acquisitions therefore range across those artists who are most representative of the movements, currents and tendencies to have emerged since the Second World War, artists who are important not only for their intrinsic quality but also because they reflect the dialogue between European and North American art. The Guggenheim Museum Bilbao has deliberately restricted itself to this period because the Solomon R. Guggenheim Museum in New York and the Peggy Guggenheim Collection in Venice both already have collections of modernist masterpieces. The Bilbao Guggenheim is also especially attentive to Basque and Spanish art in constituting its collection.

The first acquisition by the Bilbao Guggenheim, which currently holds ninety one works, was a painting by Mark Rothko, *Untitled* (1952-53), considered one of the masterpieces by this key figure of Abstract Expressionism. This movement is also represented by works from Willem de Kooning, Robert Motherwell and Clyfford Still. Linked to them, although standing very much apart because of his original development, Cy Twombly is distinguished by the recently acquired *Nine Discourses on Commodus*, the first unified ensemble by this artist and an inspiration for much of the work that followed it, which can be considered as the culmination of his explosive and expressionist early years in Italy.

In parallel to American Abstract Expressionism, Europe is marked by art informel, which was heralded in France by Jean Dubuffet, who developed the specific language of art brut. The Bilbao Guggenheim holds some major examples of Spanish informel art, with works by Antoni Tàpies and Antonio Saura.

Between Abstract Expressionism and Pop Art, which flourished in the 1960s in reaction to the dominant school of abstraction, we find the American Robert Rauschenberg, whose *Barge* (1962-63), a magisterial synthesis of his work, was acquired jointly by the Guggenheim Museum Bilbao and Solomon R. Guggenheim Foundation. Remarkable works by Andy Warhol and James Rosenquist illustrate American Pop Art.

On the European side, Nouveau Réalisme, represented by Yves Klein, occupies a choice position in the collection with a large-format canvas and an installation, *Fontaine de feu* (*Fire Fountain*, p. 12), in the Museum pool, where the public can see it in working order for the first time. Finally, Arte Povera is represented by a work from Greek artist Jannis Kounellis. Conceptual Art, Minimalism and post-Minimalism, which emerged across the Atlantic in opposition to the trends mentioned above, are illustrated by works from Sol LeWitt and Richard Serra. In 2005 the Museum commissioned from Serra *The Matter of Time*, a magnificent ensemble created specially for the big 104 Arcelor-Mittal Gallery. These seven monumental sculptures joined his *Snake* (1994-97), which was acquired by the Museum for its inaugural exhibition. *The Matter of Time* is the biggest commission from any artist in recent decades, and is also the most eloquent expression to date of Serra's approach to sculpture and relation to space. Land Art, another movement born in the United States, is represented by the work of an English exponent of the form, Richard Long, titled *Bilbao Circle* (2000).

The collection also includes a broad selection of major German artists from the second half of the twentieth century, notably Joseph Beuys, Anselm Kiefer, Sigmar Polke and Gerhard Richter. The Italian art of the Transavanguardia is illustrated by Francesco Clemente with an installation specially commissioned for the Museum's Room 203: *La Stanza della Madre (The Mother's Room,* 1995-96), plus a work by Enzo Cucchi.

The art of the 1980s and 1990s is extensively covered with Christian Boltanski, Julian Schnabel, Jean-Michel Basquiat, Gilbert & George, Jeff Koons, Jenny Holzer, Jim Dine and the Japanese artist Fujiko Nakaya, whose *Fog Sculpture no. 08 025 (F.O.G.)* (1998) visitors can admire outside. The collection gives particular prominence to Basque and Spanish art during this period, with remarkable artists like Txomin Badiola, Miquel Barceló, Cristina Iglesias, Prudencio Irazabal, Juan Luis Moraza, Juan Muñoz, Javier Pérez, Susana Solano, Francesc Torres, Darío Urzay, Juan Uslé, Pello Irazu, Koldobika Jauregi and José Mari Lazkano. Also worth emphasising is the presence of three major figures of the art of the last half-century: the Basque sculptors Jorge Oteiza and Eduardo Chillida – by whom the Museum owns a large number of works in different formats and materials – and

French artist Louise Bourgeois, with her magnificent outdoor sculpture *Maman* (1999; cast iron version, 2001). Works by Spain's leading exponent of geometrical abstraction, the painter Pablo Palazuelo, and by Miquel Navarro, one of the most important contemporary Spanish sculptors, also feature in the collection. There is, too, the sculpture *Reina Mariana* (2001) donated by Manolo Valdés, another contemporary Spanish artist of international renown.

Over the last few years, the museums of the Guggenheim network – the Solomon R. Guggenheim Museum, the Peggy Guggenheim Collection, the Guggenheim Museum, Berlin and the Guggenheim Museum, Bilbao – have helped redefine the concepts of collecting and acquiring works of art. Within this new perspective, the individual collections of the different museums are merged into a single entity. The diversity and complementarity of the artists and movements represented in each collection come together in an ensemble of such magnitude and unique wealth that it can claim to provide visitors with a real view of the art of our time. Selections from this collection are selectively exhibited in dynamic shows in a rotation designed to provide the public with multiple vantage points on modern and contemporary art, and thus to keep them coming back, while allowing the Museum to explore different perspectives on new art enhanced by an extraordinary building. ∎

Previous double page: Jeff Koons (born in York, Pennsylvania, USA, 1955), *Tulips*, 1995-2004. High chrome content stainless steel with a transparent colour coating. 2 x 4.6 x 5.2 m.

Page left: Sol LeWitt (born in Hartford, USA, 1928), *Wall Drawing no. 831 (Geometric Forms)*, 1997. Acrylic on wall. Site-specific dimensions.

Bottom left: Koldobika Jauregi (born in Alkiza, 1959), *Asedio I (Seat I)*, 2003. Engraved, carved, burnt and polychrome wood. Site-specific dimensions; relief (triptych): 310 x 550 cm; sculpture: 2.62 x 1 x 1 m.

Bottom right: Richard Long (born in Bristol, England, 1945), *Bilbao Circle*, 2000. Delabole slate. Diameter: 13 m.

Louise **Bourgeois**

Born in Paris, France, 1911

Autobiographical references tinged with resentment and
nostalgia are a constant in the work of Louise Bourgeois.
In the course of a career lasting almost six decades, she
has created rich, innovative works that oscillate between
abstraction and the visceral representation of psychic
states. Thousands of drawings, installations and
sculptures in marble, wood, metal, plaster or latex have
thus afforded glimpses of her personal experience while
at the same time illustrating the bittersweet challenge
of human life generally. *Maman*, part of a series that
the artist presents as a homage to her mother, displays
the ambiguity of motherhood: the spider uses silk not only
to make its cocoon but also to capture its prey, and its
gigantic legs form both a cage and a shelter which protects
a pouch of eggs stuck dangerously to its abdomen.

Maman,
1999 (cast 2001).
Bronze, stainless steel
and marble.
8.95 x 9.8 x 11.6m.

Jeff **Koons**

Born in York, Pennsylvania, United States, 1955

In an age when media saturation has engendered a crisis in representation, Jeff Koons sets out to 'communicate with the masses' by using the visual languages of advertising, marketing and the leisure industry. With *Puppy*, a giant West Highland terrier covered with flowering plants, he combines elitist references (the art of topiary and breeding dogs) and popular ones (decorative pottery, greetings cards). Koons conceived this public sculpture with a view to arousing optimism and inspiring, as he says, 'confidence and security'. We find the same vein in *Tulips*, a bunch of seven tulips five metres high that look like giant balloons in luminescent colours. These playful objects seem to come straight out of some wonderland. They exemplify the artist's talent for transforming something banal into a seductive object that questions the function of art within a culture of consumption. As in Koons's earlier works, irony and sincerity coexist with an acute critical sense.

Puppy,
1992.
Stainless steel, soil,
and flowering plants.
12.4 x 12.4 x 8.2 m.

32

Above:
**Die Berühmten
Orden der Nacht
(The Renowned
Orders of the Night)**,
1997. Acrylic and
emulsion on canvas.
510 x 500 cm.

Page left:
Berenice,
1989. Lead, glass,
photography, and hair.
1.2 x 3.9 x 3.2 m.

Anselm **Kiefer**
Born in Donaueschingen, Germany, 1945

Born in Germany a few months before the end of the Second World War, Anselm Kiefer
grew up with the legacy of modern warfare and witnessed the attempts to reconstruct
a divided nation and that nation's struggle for renewal. In his work, Kiefer explores
the relations between German mythology and history and their influence on the rise
of fascism. In dealing with these issues he has broken aesthetic taboos and brought
back subliminal images. His large-scale works are full of references to the tradition
of German Romanticism and to his country's political heritage. Working in an almost
monochrome palette of greys and browns, he combines paint with lead leaf, straw,
plaster, seeds, ashes and earth. After the fall of the Berlin Wall in 1989, Kiefer settled
in the South of France, where he began to explore more universal themes. While
continuing to take inspiration from religion, myth and history, he now centres his work
more on human spirituality and the workings of the mind. His very diverse subjects
range from sunflowers in Arles to the queens of France and, while still informed by
a sense of history, this new imagery has been accompanied by a new interest and
even delight in pictorial form.

Joseph **Beuys**

Krefeld, Germany, 1921 – Düsseldorf, Germany, 1986

Joseph Beuys is one of the figures who most vividly embody
the Europe of the 1970s and 1980s. He sought to focus interest
not on the artist's work but on his personality, his actions and his
opinions. In 1943, when he was a pilot in the Luftwaffe, his plane
was shot down over the Crimea. He would later claim that he was
saved by Tatars who managed to preserve his body heat by
covering him with fat and wrapping him in felt blankets. These
two materials, fat and felt, feature recurrently in his work. One of
his most theatrical installations, *Blitzschlag mit Lichtschein auf
Hirsch* (*Lightning with a Stag in Its Glare*), illustrates Beuys's
obsession with earth, animals and death.
This arrangement of mysterious objects evokes a natural setting,
possibly a clearing in a wood, where a stag (an ironing board on
wooden 'legs'), the excremental forms of 'primitive animals'
(tools stuck in a pile of clay) and a goat (a broken-down
wheelbarrow with three wheels) are illuminated by a powerful
bolt of lightning (a heavy triangular form hanging precariously
from a beam). In his work, which often has a strong political
content, Beuys champions a changed way of thinking induced
more by the individual capacity for comprehension than by
technological progress.

**Blitzschlag mit
Lichtschein auf Hirsch,
(Lightning with a Stag
in Its Glare),**
1958-85.
39 elements:
aluminium, bronze,
and iron.
Varying size.

Cy Twombly

Born in Lexington, Virginia, United States, 1928

Recognisable by his agile, gestural and seemingly random brushstrokes, Cy Twombly came out of the American Abstract Expressionist school. In 1957, however, he settled in Rome and, unlike other AbEx artists, took an interest in the classical sources of Western art – Greece, Rome and the Italian Renaissance. Thus figures from classical mythology and the sites of the Ancient World were at the centre of his abstract compositions. In the cycle *Nine Discourses on Commodus* he evokes the creative and destructive forces embodied by the Roman emperor Aurelius Commodus, with each painting showing one of his conflicts. Degeneration is expressed through the emphatic colour which, as a metaphor of a choleric mind, denotes the gradual loss of reason, until its excesses transform it into a violent and destructive convulsion. Twombly's art is about the creative unconscious: it illustrates the process whereby a mad emperor is transformed into an archetype. A close reading of Twombly's images takes us beyond the apparent chaos to the reality of the classical past.

Nine Discourses on Commodus, 1963.
Work in nine parts.
204 x 134 cm each.

Page left, from top to bottom and left to right.
Part I: oil paint, lead pencil and wax crayon on canvas.

Part II: oil paint and lead pencil on canvas.

Part III: oil paint, wax crayon and lead pencil on canvas.

Part IV: oil paint, lead pencil and wax crayon on canvas.

Part V: oil paint, wax crayon and lead pencil on canvas.

Part VI: oil paint, wax crayon and lead pencil on canvas.

Part VII: oil paint and lead pencil on canvas.

Part VIII: oil paint, wax crayon and lead pencil on canvas.

Part IX: oil paint, wax crayon and lead pencil on canvas.

Mark **Rothko**

Dvinsk, Russia, 1903 – New York, United States, 1970

Mark Rothko is one of the main representatives
of American Abstract Expressionism. This
movement was characterised by its attempt to
weld together form and emotion by focusing on
the expression of the artist's personality. In his
painting Rothko expresses the universality of
human aspirations through broad areas of colour,
a feature which led some critics to describe his
work as 'mystic'. *Untitled* is one of his biggest
canvases. It was painted at a time when the
artist was limiting his compositions to three
horizontal rectangles of variable proportions which
he painted by combining a choice of colours.
His broad bands of colour produce a feeling
of immateriality. Rothko gives his paint a downy
texture that makes it seem nebulous and light.
The rectangles seem to float above the canvas.
Rothko superimposes very fine layers of paint
so as to let the underlayers show through, as if
a hidden source of light was appearing from the
back of the painting, so as to seize and envelop
the beholder.

Untitled,
1952-53.
Oil on canvas.
300 x 442.5 cm.

Robert **Rauschenberg**

Born in Port Arthur, Texas, United States, 1925

Robert Rauschenberg started using the silkscreen painting technique
in the early 1960s. Whereas other processes oblige the artist to keep
the reproduced image at its original size, this technique makes it possible
to transpose images to any scale. *Barge* is one of the best examples of
this. As is frequently the case in Rauschenberg's work, this series draws
abundantly on images from magazines and photographic archives as well
as the artist's own photographs, which are transferred at different scales
onto serigraphic screens. This kind of painting, which combines both
the themes and the techniques of the mass media, prompted critics
at the time to associate Rauschenberg with Pop Art. However, his work is
a long way from the cold, serial kind of production characteristic of that
movement. It is in effect more gestural, more craftsmanlike, and manifests
great expressivity, which is particularly visible in the hand-painted areas,
in the superimposition of images, in certain collages and in the deliberate
mistakes in the silkscreening process.

Barge,
1962-63.
Oil and silkscreened
ink on canvas.
203 x 980 cm.
Guggenheim Bilbao
Museoa and Solomon
R. Guggenheim
Museum, New York.

Richard **Serra**

Born in San Francisco, United States, 1939

When he set eyes on the plans of the huge hall where he was going to install his work, Californian artist Richard Serra, a master of post-Minimalist sculpture and a great friend of Frank Gehry's, responded enthusiastically. In what he called 'the great hall', he began in 1997 by installing *Snake*, a work 31 metres long and 4 metres high, weighing 180 tons. In 2004 it was joined by seven colossal sculptures that had been commissioned from the artist to form his monumental work *The Matter of Time*. This permanent installation stands as a benchmark of Serra's formal development. When visitors walk through these sculptures they unexpectedly seem to change, creating a vertiginous and unforgettable moving space. The corridors reveal unsuspected dimensions. As when walking through a medieval city, chronological time and the time of experience, which fixes the fragments of visual and physical memories, combine and regenerate.

Left:
Blind Spot Reversed,
2003-05.
Weathering steel, three
torus and three spherical
sections.
Overall: 4 x 17.2 x 9 m;
plate thickness: 5 cm.

Page right:
Snake,
1994-97.
Weatherproof steel,
three units, each
comprised of two
conical sections,
4 x 31.7 x 7.84 m.

Following double page:
panoramic view of
The Matter of Time,
1993-2005.

Jenny **Holzer**

Born in Gallipolis, United States, 1950

This installation by the American conceptual artist
Jenny Holzer was conceived and made specially for
a room in the Bilbao Guggenheim. The work consists
of a series of luminous letters or LED screens of the
kind generally used for commercial display in public
space. Holzer uses this support to communicate
her disturbing messages to an unsuspecting public
and thus challenge their way of looking at things.
At the front of the work, the messages in English
and Spanish crawl across the screen in red letters
on vertical strips a meter apart, while on the other
side the same text appears in blue letters in Euskera,
the Basque language. This 'hidden' text illustrates
the relation between Basque culture and the outside
world. Holzer has also painted messages on the walls
and ceiling of the room in a shiny grey colour that
reflects and deforms the messages. This effect is
perceptible throughout the gallery space, heightening
the contrast between the right angles of the signage
and the curve of the walls around it.

Installation for Bilbao,
1997.
Electronic LED sign
columns.
Site-specific dimensions.

Miquel **Barceló**
Born in Felanitx, Spain, 1957

Above:
El diluvio (Flood),
1990.
Mixed media on canvas.
230 x 285 cm.

Page left:
**Cabrit i cabrida
(Male and Female Goats),**
1992.
Mixed media on canvas.
297 x 246 cm.
Gift, Galerie
Bruno Bischofberger.

Miquel Barceló is one of the best-known young Spanish artists on the International scene. From Paris to Majorca via Mali, he reinterprets traditional genres (landscapes, still lifes and interiors), combining them with autobiographical elements in large-format works. Barceló makes frequent use of materials found in his place of work and uses techniques that imprint a pronounced texture on the surface. He is constantly experimenting and innovating in his techniques of composition, his use of perspective, colour, light, materials and textures. His regular sojourns in Gao (Mali) since the late 1980s have had an enduring impact on his life and work. It was there that he began to emphasise the textural aspect of painting and confer a new, almost mystical value on matter. He has indeed said that Africa helped him to 'clean' his art, to throw off the weighty cultural burden that had previously marked his style. As a result, his themes have become simpler, centring on light, life and death. *Cabrit i cabrida* (*Male and Female Goats*), is part of a series made in the early 1990s showing hanged or sacrificed animals. This work, which brings to mind the classical still lifes of Sánchez Cotán and the flayed animals of Rembrandt, has sometimes been linked to animist ritual.

Antoni **Tàpies**

Born in Barcelona, Spain, 1923

In the years that followed the Second World War, the European and American art scenes witnessed the emergence of an essentially abstract form of painting that focused essentially on materials, expression, gesture and brushstroke. The Americans called this tendency Abstract Expressionism, while in France the tendency was dubbed art informel – literally, art without form – or, for, some variants, Tachism (from the French word *tache*, meaning stain or mark). Antoni Tàpies was associated with Tachism because of the very rich textures and accumulations of colour that seemed to coexist accidentally in his canvases. Giving pride of place to modest materials, whether natural, such as sand or straw, or manmade, such as rope and fabric, Tàpies revealed the unexpected beauty found in overlooked places. He thinks of his works, whose large size is conducive to contemplation, as objects that will inspire the beholder's thoughts in accordance with their own experience. The two panels of *Ambrosía* evoke ageing walls soiled by human use.

Ambrosía (Ambrosia),
1989.
Mixed media on canvas.
200 x 600 cm.

Robert **Motherwell**

Aberdeen, Washington, United States, 1915 – Provincetown, Massachusetts, United States, 1991

Motherwell was one only 21 when the Spanish Civil War broke out, but the atrocities
of the conflict made a deep impression on him. Years later, he would devote a series
of over two hundred works to this theme, each work entitled *Elegy to the Spanish
Republic,* in a homage to human suffering and as a kind of abstract and poetic symbol
of the inexorable cycle of life and death. Motherwell's allusion to human mortality
through a non-referential visual language demonstrates his admiration for French
Symbolism. The dialectical nature of life is expressed through the juxtaposition
of white and black. A great many of Motherwell's works, like those in the *Iberia* series,
begun in 1958, are almost entirely black. Motherwell made the following commentary
on his *Elegies*: 'After a period of painting them, I discovered black as one of my subjects
– and with black, the contrasting white, a sense of life and death which to me is quite
Spanish.' The meaning of each work in this series begun in 1948 with an ink sketch
illustrating a poem by Harold Rosenberg is subjective and evolves over time.

Iberia,
1958. Oil on canvas.
179 x 226.5 cm.

Gerhard **Richter**

Born in Dresden, Germany, 1932

Gerhard Richter has stated, 'I am suspicious regarding the image of reality which our senses convey to us and which is incomplete and limited', and his insistence on the illusionistic nature of painting has led to a painterly practice that emphasises the mediated experience of reality by incorporating imagery based on found and familiar photographs. Photographs provide a pretext for a painting, injecting a measure of objectivity and eliminating the processes of apprehension and interpretation. In *Seestück* (*Seascape*), Richter combines various tropes of painting and photography to create a kind of representational problem: how and when does the eye sense the difference between a painted surface and the photographically recorded? In this seemingly conventional, large-scale work, the pigment is thinly applied, resulting in a surface that emulates the flatness of a photograph. And, as a snapshot might be, it is blurred, literally obscuring the distinction between the photographic and the painted. Here Richter draws from sources both traditional (the moody, atmospheric landscapes of the German Romantic painter Caspar David Friedrich) and popular (holiday snapshots) to achieve this meditation on the nature of looking.

Yves **Klein**

Nice, France, 1928 – Paris, France, 1962

Judo was Yves Klein's great passion, and he even became a black belt in Tokyo. However, when he realized that the French Judo Federation was not going to give him the support he was hoping for, he decided to change direction and dedicate himself to his second passion: art. During the seven years that followed, Klein produced an extremely varied and complex set of works ranging from monochromes to mural reliefs and fire paintings. He became famous for his prominent use of a paint made with a powdery cobalt pigment which he patented under the name 'International Klein Blue'. According to Klein, IKB represented the physical manifestation of the invisible cosmic energy that was floating in the air. For his *Anthropométries* series Klein used naked women whose bodies had been coated with paint as his brushes. His idea of getting them to press their bodies against paper (which he would later mount on canvas) cancelled any illusion of a third dimension in pictorial space. Even today, there is still a degree of perplexity about his work, with uncertainty as to whether Klein sincerely believed in the mystic capacities of the artist or was satirizing the metaphysical proclivities of many modern painters and at the same time deriding the art market.

La Grande
**Anthropométrie bleue
(ANT 105) [Large Blue
Anthropometry
(ANT 105)],**
ca. 1960.
Blue pigment
and synthetic resin
on paper on canvas.
280 x 428 cm.

Fujiko **Nakaya**

Born in Sapporo, Japan, 1933

Fujiko Nakaya was the first artist to use fog as a material. This was a radical innovation both technologically and in terms of art history. Her vision of natural ephemera and sense of experimentation were of considerable importance to conceptual art, Land Art and, more particularly, light-based art. *Fog Sculpture no. 08 025 (F.O.G.)* is an atmospheric sculpture created using an artificially generated fog that immediately forms a shape when it enters into contact with the microclimate for which it was created. Its constantly changing shape explores in real time the meteorological and topographic conditions of the environment, reflecting the delicate equilibrium and dynamic process of the exchanges found in nature. If Fujiko Nakaya is noteworthy for her art of 'collaborating' with the elements (water, the atmosphere, drafts, time, etc.) in order to create sculptures, she is also internationally renowned for her pioneering work in video art and for her activism on behalf of women's rights and ecological causes.

Fog Sculpture no. 08 025 (F.O.G.), 1998. Water-fog generated by 1,000 fog nozzles and high-pressure pump/motor system. Site-specific dimensions.

Jorge **Oteiza**

Orio, Spain, 1908 – San Sebastian, Spain, 2003

In 1947, after a long sojourn in South America, and having assimilated
the impact of Henry Moore's work, Oteiza worked in the Basque Country,
developing what he would call his 'experimental propositions'. This work
was the result of a series of conceptual postulates such as the one that
every artistic practice starts with a nothingness that is null and attains
a nothingness that is everything. Thus, a sculpture that is initially expressive,
in front of which the spectator is purely receptive, is succeeded by a stage
in which expression is annihilated, the material is 'de-occupied', when the
predominant role is played by space and, consequently, by a beholder who is
henceforth active in relation to the emptiness of the sculpture. In 1958,
Oteiza began his 'works of conclusion', geometrical forms so pared down
that they are now seen as forerunners of Minimalism, such as his *Cajas vacías*
(*Empty Boxes*). In 1959 Oteiza gave up sculpture to devote himself to
cultural, political and educational research in the Basque Country.

Page left:
Caja vacía con gran apertura (Empty Box with Large Opening),
1958. Forged steel.
46 x 45 x 39 cm.

Above:
Hillargia,
1957. Steel.
34 x 35 x 40 cm.

Eduardo **Chillida**

San Sebastian, Spain, 1924 – San Sebastian, Spain, 2002

Chillida made his first sculptures in stone and plaster but soon moved on to iron, wood and steel, all of which materials are associated with the agriculture and traditional industry of the Basque Country, and evoke the 'black light' of his native land. The work *Consejo al espacio V* (*Advice to Space V*), made wholly of steel, is a meditation on the different ways of experiencing and interpreting infinite space and depth. By translating his vision of space into an abstract material form, Chillida explores density, scale and rhythm. His interest in the relation between light and architecture dates back to his travels in Greece and Italy during the 1960s. He consequently began using alabaster for its luminous, if veiled quality and its ability to reveal and hide at the same time, a bit like the obscure and nebulous atmospheric light of his homeland. In *Lo profundo es el aire* (*How Profound Is the Air*) the rough-hewn finish of the stone is combined with a polished, architectonic interior space. The title illustrates the sculptor's position in relation to space or air, which for him is a material that is just as vital as stone or wood.

Above:
**Consejo al espacio V
(Advice to Space V),**
1993. Steel.
3.05 x 1.43 x 2.07 m.

Page right:
**Lo profundo es el aire
(How Profound Is the Air),**
1996. Alabaster.
0.94 x 1.22 x 1.24 m.

The first death in a bomb explosion in 1968, the industrial crisis and the violence and civil repression of the last years of the Franco regime coincided with the appearance of a new artistic generation whose avant-garde convictions and political engagement were similar to those of its predecessors, but were formulated in a less optimistic, more self-critical context. Thus, in the late 1970s a group of artists emerged on the Basque scene who, if still influenced by Conceptual Art and Minimalism, called into question the aesthetic and ideological postulates of the past, precisely when art was undergoing a major crisis of representation. This phenomenon was paralleled by the growing cultural self-affirmation of Spain's autonomous regions. These new artistic generations with a link to regionalism were immediately taken up, indeed, by the cultural institutions. The collection of the Guggenheim Museum Bilbao features a coherent ensemble of works associated with what is known as the new Basque sculpture, by artists such as Cristina Iglesias, Txomin Badiola, Pello Irazu and Juan Luis Moraza, who set out to rethink sculpture by combining the modernist tradition with a deconstruction of historical myths and a search for new formal solutions. Appearing in the 1990s, and in a more international context, the work of Javier Pérez marked an aesthetic turning point: it questions human identity and man's biological condition, addressing issues of a more existential nature at the secularised century's end.

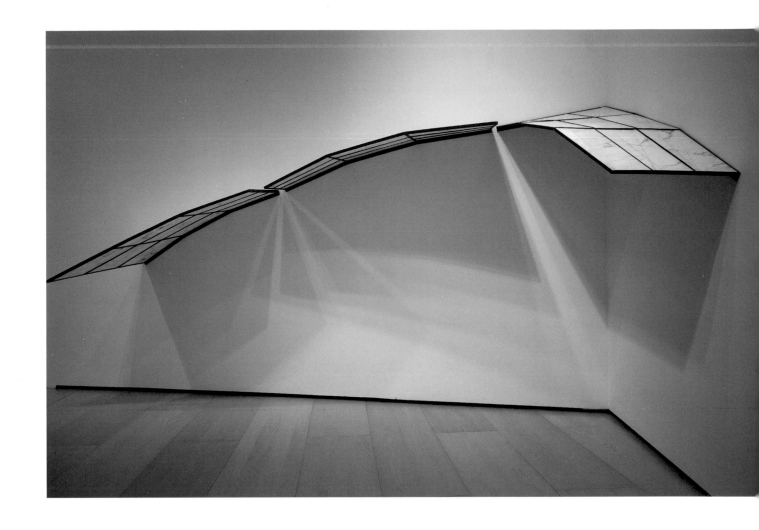

Cristina **Iglesias**

Born in San Sebastian, Spain, 1956

Page left:
**Sin título (Celosia II)
[Untitled (Jealousy II)]**,
1997.
Wood, resin, and
bronze powder.
2.6 x 3.5 x 3 m.

Above:
**Sin título (Habitación
de alabastro) [Untitled
(Alabaster Room)]**,
1993. Iron and alabaster.
Site specific dimensions.

Cristina Iglesias is one of the most internationally prominent contemporary Basque
artists. Fusing the organic and the industrial in a great variety of compositions,
her large-scale works encourage beholders to walk around and sometimes through
their structures. Iglesias likes to work on the edge of abstraction, using details that can
be thought to have a narrative burden. *Sin título (Celosía II) [Untitled (Jealousy II)]*,
made in 1997, is an exotic-looking construction that, while appearing to be closed,
in fact offers several points of access. This work evokes Arab mashrabiyahs, those
screens through which women can look without being seen. As in many of her works,
the artist here manages to combine apparently contradictory contents: the piece is
as much a prison as a refuge. The panels that form this work were made using delicate
geometrical drawings. Here and there we can read sentences in Spanish: according to
Iglesias, this effect 'is part of the mystery. I really like hidden meanings. We know
they are there and yet we can hardly see them'.

Javier **Pérez**
Born in Bilbao, Spain, 1968

Levitas,
1998. Blown glass.
Site specific dimensions.

Txomin **Badiola**
Born in Bilbao, Spain, 1957

**Complot de familia,
Segunda versión (Family
Plot, Second Version),**
1993-95.
Wood, glass, rope, and
two photographs.
Site-specific dimensions.

Pello **Irazu**

Born in Donostia-San Sebastian,
Spain, 1963

Life Forms 304,
2003.
Iron, plywood, wood
and adhesive tape.
Mural painting.
Dimensions of
the construction:
360 x 315 x 340 cm;
overall: site-specific
dimensions.

Juan Luis **Moraza**

Born in Vitoria-Gasteiz, Spain, 1960

**Éxtasis, Status, Estatua
(Ecstasy, Status, Statue),**
1994. Synthetic resin.
10 x 400 x 400 cm.

Visitor information

Museo Guggenheim Bilbao
Guggenheim Museum, Bilbao
Abandoibarra Et. 2. – 48001 Bilbao.
www.guggenheim-bilbao.es
Information:
Phone.: (+34) 944 35 90 80
Fax: (+34) 944 35 90 39
informacion@guggenheimbilbao.es

Opening hours
Tuesday to Sunday, 10:00–20:00.
Closed Monday, except in July
and August. Closed 25 December
and 1 January. Closure at 17:00
on 24 and 31 December.
Ticketing ends half an hour before
closing time. Visitors are asked to
leave the Museum starting at 19:45.

Access
• Practical access by tramway.
• Car: municipal parking near the
museum.
Information: (+34) 944 35 90 80.
• Free wheelchairs, buggies and
portable chairs specially designed
for museum visitors.

Rates
• Concessionary rates for pensioners
and students.
• Free admission for children under
12 and Friends of the Museum.
• Tickets valid for the whole day,
even if visitors momentarily leave
the Museum.

Advance purchase of tickets
Advance tickets can be bought from
the Museum or from the BBK and
Servicaixa multiservice machines
of La Caixa (vouchers available from
the desk for Friends of the Museum).

Group access
• Special access for groups with
reservations on the river facade.
• For groups of over twenty,
authorisation must be obtained from
the Groups service: (+34) 944 35 90 23,
open Monday to Friday, 9:00–14:00.
Reservations limited.

Friends of the Museum
Phone: (+34) 944 35 90 14
Monday to Friday, 9:00–14:00.
amigos@guggenheim-bilbao.es

Guided tours
• Guided tours of the permanent
collection and temporary exhibitions
at set hours or by appointment from
Tuesday to Sunday at 11:00, 12:30,
16:30 and 18:30.
Enrolment half an hour before the
tour begins at the Information
counter. Maximum: 20 persons.
• Free guided tours for the disabled.
• Tours in sign language for the hard
of hearing.
• Tactile tours for the visually impaired.
• Tours for the mentally handicapped.
• Maximum group size: 15.
Booking is essential.
Information and bookings:
Monday to Friday, 9:00–14:00.
Phone: (+34) 944 35 90 90
Fax: (+34) 944 35 90 39
Reserve a guide: Monday to Friday,
9:00–14:00: (+34) 944 35 90 90

Audioguides
• Available in many languages: Basque,
Spanish, English, French, German
and Italian.
• For the deaf, videoguide in PDA
form for the work by Richard Serra,
The Matter of Time, and tape loop
in the Auditorium.
• Audioguide for children: no. 100,
for *The Matter of Time*.

Boutique-bookshop
The boutique and bookstore
of the Guggenheim Museum,
Bilbao offers a wide choice of quality
articles and publications relating to
the Guggenheim collections,
the temporary exhibitions, avant-garde
design and modern and contemporary
art. It offers exclusive designs by
prestigious artists, some of them
specially created by the Guggenheim
Museums in relation to exhibitions.
Tel.: (+34) 944 35 90 85.

Library
Specialist library on modern and
contemporary art, with an emphasis
on the Guggenheim Bilbao collection.
Online access to the computerised
catalogue and to documentation
relating to the Museum collections,
temporary shows and artists.

Guggenheim Bilbao restaurant
• Run by the team of prestigious
restaurateur Martin Berasategui, the
restaurant offers visitors the chance
to enjoy one of the most personal
takes on Basque cuisine now available.

The Guggenheim Bilbao boutique-bookshop.

The Guggenheim Bilbao café.